Yor

MW01171562

Short and Fun Japanese Stories in Hiragana and Basic Kanji

Clay & Yumi Boutwell

www.TheJapanShop.com
www.TheJapanesePage.com
www.MakotoPlus.com

INTRODUCTION

読んでみよう can serve as an invitation to read together with
someone or signify a personal intention to give reading something
a try. Embrace both interpretations and let Yonde Miyo-! guide
your language learning journey.

Whether you've just mastered hiragana and seek practice, or if
you're looking to enhance your reading comprehension of both
hiragana and kanji, this book is tailored for you.If you are a
beginner to upper beginner of Japanese, this new collection of
stories is here to the rescue!

Read real Japanese—beginner level but not boring Japanese!
You won't find the Japanese version of Dick and Jane, but you will
find stories written for adults. Enjoy reading flash fiction, super
short informative essays, and funny stories of common mistakes
made by learners of Japanese.

Best of all, the only requirement is that you can read hiragana
and have a very basic understanding of Japanese. Vocabulary and
grammar will be defined and explained.

The format is a little different from our other more advanced
readers. The idea is for the reader **to read the entire story three
times.** Each page will have a sentence or two in hiragana *(with
spaces between words for you to see "words" instead of syllables)*
at the top and that same content in full Japanese *(with furigana—
small hiragana over kanji)* at the bottom. The middle will have the
glossary and grammatical explanations. Lastly, the story is
presented again in Japanese without furigana. See if you can read
it after going through the previous two versions and explanations.

If you have just learned hiragana, you may want to listen to the
sound file while reading the top hiragana section to practice

correct pronunciation. If you have studied Japanese a bit longer, you may want to start with the bottom version and take note of the glossary for understanding.

The glossary will have the word as it appears in the story, but it will also give the "dictionary" form so you can look the word up further.

Fun in language learning not only boosts motivation but also prevents the pitfalls of inconsistency. A single skipped day of study can easily snowball into a week, or worse, an indefinite hiatus. And so, we hope you will have as much fun reading these stories as we had writing them.

About Japanese Pronunciation

As a quick and dirty guide, pronounce the consonants as you would in English. The vowels are like the vowel sounds in Spanish.

- a (ah) as in 'father'
- i (ii) as in 'pizza'
- u (oo) as in 'food'
- e (eh) as in 'bet'
- (oh) as in 'orange'

See the last page to download sound files for all the Stories found in the book.

ABOUT CLAY & YUMI

Yumi was a popular radio DJ in Japan for over ten years. She has extensive training in standard Japanese pronunciation which makes her perfect for creating these language instructional audio files.

Meanwhile, Clay has been a passionate learner of Japanese for many years now. His free language learning website, www.TheJapanesePage.com, got its start back in 1999 as a way to help other learners of Japanese as well as himself.

In 2002, they opened www.TheJapanShop.com, a resource for students of Japanese to access hard-to-find Japanese books.

Yumi and I are **very grateful** for your purchase and we truly hope this book will help you improve your Japanese. **We love our customers and don't take a single one of you for granted.** If you have any questions about this book or Japanese in general, please feel free to contact us via email or on our social media platforms.

Clay & Yumi Boutwell (and Makoto & Megumi) in Fukui, Japan
https://TheJapanShop.com
https://TheJapanesePage.com
https://MakotoPlus.com

Table of Contents

Story 1 Taiyaki

日本のストリートフード「たい焼き」

Japanese Street Food: "taiyaki"

| Normal Speed | Slow Speed |

- 日本のストリートフード *nihon no sutori-to fu-do*—street food in Japan; street food of Japan; Japanese street food [日本 (Japan) + の (of; in; 's; modifier) + ストリートフード (street food)]

- 「たい焼き」 「*taiyaki*」 —"taiyaki" [a Japanese fish-shaped cake filled with red bean paste]

As a reminder, the top and bottom Japanese texts are identical in meaning. The top version is only in hiragana and includes spaces between words. The bottom version has no spaces and uses kanji with furigana.

Unless you are just practicing hiragana recognition, try to work through both versions to improve reading speed, reading comprehension, listening comprehension, vocabulary, kanji, and grammar. If you don't feel confident in your understanding, review the English translation at the end.

たい と.いう さかな の かたち を した
おかし で、

- 鯛という魚 *tai to iu sakana*—a fish called *tai* [鯛 (*tai*; sea bream; species of reddish-brown Pacific sea bream) + という (that; called; is used to define, describe, and generally just talk about the thing itself) + 魚 (fish)]

- 鯛という魚の形をしたお菓子で *tai to iu sakana no katachi o shita okashi de*—a pancake that is shaped like a fish called *tai* (sea bream) and [鯛という魚 (a fish called *tai*) + の (modifier) + 形 (form; shape; figure) + を (indicates the direct object of action) + した (plain past form of する (to do)) + お菓子 (sweet treat; cake; confectionery) + で (て-form of です (be; is) which is used to connect the next phrase, creating the meaning of "and")]

鯛という魚の形をしたお菓子で、

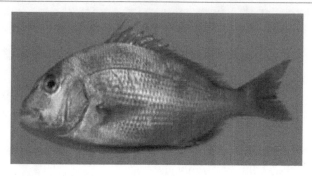

Pagrus major Red seabream ja01.jpg - Wikimedia Commons

なか に あんこ が たっぷり はいって いま
す。

- 中に *naka ni*—inside [中 (inside; interior; in) + に (expresses the location of existence)]

- あんこがたっぷりはいっています *anko ga tappuri haitte imasu*—is well-filled with *anko* (red bean jam); be loaded with *anko* [あんこ (*anko*; red bean paste; red bean jam) + が (identifies what performs the action; emphasizes the preceding word) + たっぷり (full; in plenty; ample) + はいっています (is filled; is contained; ています-form of はいる (to contain; to go into) which is used to describe the actual condition or appearance of the subject; how to form: Verb て-form + います)]

中にあんこがたっぷりはいっています。

めいじ　じだい　から　たべられて　います。

- 明治時代から *meiji jidai kara*—since the Meiji era (1868 - 1912) [明治 (Meiji (1868-1912)) + 時代 (period; era) + から (from (e.g. time, place, numerical quantity); since)]

- 食べられています *taberarete imasu*—has/have been eaten; is/are eaten [ています-form of 食べられる (plain passive positive form of 食べる (to eat)) which is used to describe a continuous action]

明治時代から食べられています。

あんこ　の　かわり　に、くりーむ、ちょこれー
と、きゃらめる　など　が　はいって　いる　こ
　　　　　と　も　あります。

- あんこのかわりに *anko no kawari ni*—instead of *anko* [あんこ (*anko*; red bean paste; red bean jam) + の (of; modifier) + かわりに (instead of; in place of; as a substitute for)]

- クリーム *kuri-mu*—cream

- チョコレート *chokore-to*—chocolate

- キャラメル *kyarameru*—caramel (soft candy)

- など *nado*—et cetera; etc.; and the like; and so forth

- が入っていることもあります *ga haitte iru koto mo arimasu*—is sometimes filled (with cream, chocolate, etc.) [が (identifies what performs the action) + 入っている (is filled; ている-form of 入る (to contain; to go into) which is used to describe the actual condition or appearance of the subject) + こともあります (ます/polite form of こともある (sometimes do); how to form: Verb (dictionary form) + こともあります)]

あんこのかわりに、クリーム、チョコレート、キ
ャラメルなどが入っていることもあります。

あにめ「かのん」で、つきみや あゆ が たい
やき を たべて いた こと で、かいがい
でも ゆうめい に なりました。

- アニメ「かのん」で *anime 「kanon」de*—in the anime "Kanon" [アニメ (anime; animated cartoon; animated film; animation) + 「かのん」("Kanon";「」(quotation marks; " ") + かのん (Kanon)) + で (in; indicates location)]

- 月宮あゆが *tsukimiya ayu ga*—Tsukimiya Ayu [月宮あゆ (Tsukimiya Ayu) + が (identifies who performs the action)]

- たい焼きを食べていた *taiyaki o tabete ita*—ate *taiyaki*; was/were eating *taiyaki* [たい焼き (taiyaki) + を (direct object marker) + 食べていた (from 食べる (to eat); ~ていた is used to describe a continuous action happening in the past; how to form: Verb て-form + いた)]

- ことで *koto de*—by doing this [to highlight a method]

- 海外でも *kaigai demo*—even abroad

- 有名になりました *yuumei ni narimashita*—became famous [有名 (famous) + に (expresses the result of change) + なりました (became; polite past form of なる (to become; to turn; to reach; to attain))]

アニメ「かのん」で、月宮あゆがたい焼きを食
べていたことで、海外でも有名になりました。

あにめ　の　しゅじんこう　が　おいしそう　に
たべて　いる　と、

- アニメの主人公が *anime no shujinkou ga*—the main character in the anime [アニメ (anime; animation; animated cartoon) + の (of; in; modifier) + 主人公 (hero; heroine; main character; protagonist) + が (identifies who performs the action)]

- おいしそうに食べている *oishisou ni tabete iru*—is/are eating it with relish [おいしそうに (with relish; tastily; に is added to おいしそう (delicious-looking) to turn it into an adverbial form) + 食べている (is/are eating; ている-form of 食べる (to eat) which is used to describe an ongoing action)]

- と *to*—when; if

アニメの主人公がおいしそうに食べていると、

じぶん　も　たべて　みたく　なります　よ　ね。

- 自分 *jibun*—oneself; myself; yourself; himself; herself; you; I; me

- も *mo*—too; also; as well

- 食べてみたくなります *tabete mitaku narimasu*—(it) makes (you) want to try to eat [from 食べる (to eat); 食べてみたく (continuative form of 食べてみたい (want to try to eat; ~てみたい is used to express that you want to try to do something for the first time which would imply that you will see if you like it or not) which is used to connect to the next verb なります) + なります (ます/polite form of なる (make; get into; become))]

- よね *yo ne*—isn't that right? [a sentence ender which is used when you are less sure about opinions, information or knowledge]

自分も食べてみたくなりますよね。

にほん　に　きたら、ぜひ　たべて　みて　ください。

- 日本に来たら *nihon ni kitara*—when (you) come to Japan [日本 (Japan) + に (to; expresses the direction and destination) + 来たら (from 来る (to come); ~たら means "when ~; if; after"; how to form: Verb (た form) + ら)]

- ぜひ *zehi*—certainly; without fail; please; definitely

- 食べてみてください *tabete mite kudasai*—try eating (it); please try to eat [from 食べる (to eat); ~てみてください is used to express a demand, suggestion to someone to do something for the first time; how to form: Verb て-form + みてください]

日本に来たら、ぜひ食べてみてください。

REVIEW

Now, review core vocabulary before trying to read the story in natural Japanese (no furigana or spaces) on the next page.

- 日本のストリートフード *nihon no sutori-to fudo*—street food in Japan; Japanese street food

- 「たい焼き」 *「taiyaki」* —"taiyaki" [a Japanese fish-shaped cake filled with red bean paste]

- あんこがたっぷりはいっています *anko ga tappuri haitte imasu*—is well-filled with *anko* (red bean jam)

- クリーム *kuri-mu*—cream

- チョコレート *chokore-to*—chocolate

- キャラメル *kyarameru*—caramel (soft candy)

- 海外 *kaigai*—abroad; overseas

- 主人公 *shujinkou*—main character; protagonist

- ぜひ *zehi*—certainly; without fail; please; definitely

THE STORY

Now, let's read the story once more in natural Japanese.

鯛という魚の形をしたお菓子で、中にあんこがたっぷりはいっています。明治時代から食べられています。

あんこのかわりに、クリーム、チョコレート、キャラメルなどがはいっていることもあります。

アニメ「かのん」で、月宮あゆがたい焼きを食べていたことで、海外でも有名になりました。アニメの主人公がおいしそうに食べていると、自分も食べてみたくなりますよね。日本に来たら、ぜひ食べてみてください。

ENGLISH

Lastly, check the English translation to make sure you understand.

Taiyaki is a pancake that is shaped like a fish called "tai (sea bream)" and filled full of anko (sweet red bean jam). It has been eaten since the Meiji era (1868 - 1912).

Instead of anko, it is sometimes filled with cream, chocolate, caramel, etc.

Taiyaki became famous even abroad when Tsukimiya Ayu ate it in the anime "Kanon". When the main character in an anime is eating it with relish, it makes you want to try it too, right? When you come to Japan, you should definitely try one.

Story 2 Mitarashi Dango

日本のストリートフード

「みたらし団子」

Japanese Street Food: Mitarashi Dango

Normal Speed

Slow Speed

Mitarashi dango by denver935.jpg - Wikimedia Commons

こんかい　は、「みたらし　だんご」を　ごしょ
うかい　します。

- 日本のストリートフード nihon no sutori-to fu-do—street food in Japan; street food of Japan; Japanese street food [日本 (Japan) + の (of; in; 's; modifier) + ストリートフード (street food)]

- その 3 sono san—Part III

- 「みたらし団子」「mitarashi dango」—"mitarashi dango" [「」(quotation marks; " ") + みたらし団子 (mitarashi dango; skewered rice dumplings in a sweet soy glaze)]

- 今回は konkai wa—this time [今回 (this time; now) + は (adds emphasis)]

- 「みたらし団子」をご紹介します 「mitarashi dango」o goshoukai shimasu—(we) will introduce "mitarashi dango" [「みたらし団子」("mitarashi dango") + を (indicates the direct object of action) + ご紹介します (let (me) introduce; introduce; ご (honorific/polite/humble prefix) + 紹介します (introduce; bring on; induct))]

今回は、「みたらし団子」をご紹介します。

にほん　の　すとりーと　ふーど　で　とても
ながい　れきし　が　あります。

- 日本のストリートフード *nihon no sutori-to fu-do*—street food in Japan; street food of Japan; Japanese street food

- で *de*—(て-form of copula です (be; is) which is used to connect two or three sentences)

- とても *totemo*—very; awfully; exceedingly

- 長い *nagai*—long (distance, length)

- 歴史 *rekishi*—history

- (が)あります *(ga) arimasu*—there is (non-living things) [how to form: Noun + (が)あります]

日本のストリートフードでとても長い歴史があ
ります。

みたらし だんご は、ちいさな まるい だん ご です。よん こ から ご こ、くし に さして やきます。

- みたらし団子 *mitarashi dango*—mitarashi dango

- は *wa*—(indicates the sentence topic)

- 小さな *chiisana*—small; little; tiny

- 丸い *marui*—round; circular; spherical

- 団子 *dango*—dango; dumpling (usually sweet)

- です *desu*—be; is

- 4個から 5個 *yon ko kara go ko*—4pcs to 5pcs [4個 (4pcs; 個 (counter for articles)) + から (from) + 5個 (5 pcs)]

- 串にさして焼きます *kushi ni sashite yakimasu*—grilled on a skewer; roast (dumplings) on skewer [串 (spit; skewer) + に (on) + さして (て-form of さす (to pierce; to stick; to thrust) which is used to connect to the next verb 焼きます) + 焼きます (polite/ます form of 焼く (to roast; to grill))]

みたらし団子は、小さな丸い団子です。4個から5個、串にさして焼きます。

それ から、あまからい たれ を かけます。
とても おいしい です よ。みたらし だんご
は きょうと で はじまりました。

- それから *sore kara*—and then; after that

- 甘辛いたれをかけます *amakarai tare o kakemasu*—top with a sweet and salty sauce [甘辛いたれ (sweet and salty sauce; salty-sweet sauce) + を (indicates the direct object of action) + かけます (polite/ます form of かける (to put on top of; to spread; to cover))]

- とてもおいしい *totemo oishii*—very delicious [とても (very) + おいしい (good(-tasting); delicious; tasty)]

- ですよ *desu yo*—(sentence ender showing assertion or confidence)

- 京都で始まりました *kyouto de hajimarimashita*—originated in Kyoto [京都 (Kyoto (city, prefecture)) + で (in; at; indicates the location of action) + 始まりました (originated; polite past form of 始まる (to originate; to begin; to start))]

それから、甘辛いたれをかけます。とてもおい
しいですよ。
みたらし団子は京都で始まりました。

きょうと　の　ある　まつり　で　みたらし　だんご　が　とても　ゆうめい　に　なりました。

- 京都のある祭りで kyouto no aru matsuri de—at a festival in Kyoto [京都 (Kyoto (city, prefecture)) + の (of; modifier) + ある (to exist; is used to indicate the existence of inanimate objects) + 祭り (festival; feast) + で (at; indicates the location of action)]

- が ga—(identifies what performs the action; emphasizes the preceding word みたらし団子 (mitarashi dango))

- とても有名になりました totemo yuumei ni narimashita—became very famous [とても (very; awfully; exceedingly) + 有名 (famous) + に (expresses the result of change) + なりました (became; polite past form of なる (to become; to reach))]

- なりました (became; polite past form of なる (to become; to turn; to reach; to attain))]

京都のある祭りでみたらし団子がとても有名になりました。

この　まつり　は　へいあん　じだい　から　あ
ります。みたらし　だんご　も　せん　ねん　い
じょう　の　れきし　が　ある　こと　に　なり
ます。

- この祭りは kono matsuri wa—this festival [この (this) + 祭り (festival; feast) + は (indicates the sentence topic)]

- 平安時代からあります heian jidai kara arimasu—has been around since the Heian period (794 - 1185) [平安時代 (Heian period (794-1185)) + から (from; since) + あります (polite/ます form of ある (to exist; to be))]

- も mo—also (emphasizes the preceding word)

- 千年以上の歴史がある sen nen ijou no rekishi ga aru—have a history of more than 1,000 years [千年 (millennium; one thousand years; 千 (1,000; thousand) + 年 (year)) + 以上 (... and over; ... and above; ... and upwards; ... or more) + の (of; modifier) + 歴史 (history) + が (identifies what performs the action) + ある (to have; to be; to exist)]

- ことになります koto ni narimasu—it turns out that ... [how to form: Verb (dictionary form) + ことになります]

この祭りは平安時代からあります。みたらし
団子も千年以上の歴史があることになります。

「みたらし　だんご」にほん　に　きたら、ぜひ たべて　みて　ください。

- 日本に来たら *nihon ni kitara*—if (you) come to Japan [日本 (Japan) + に (to; expresses the direction and destination) + 来たら (from 来る (to come; plain form is "ku" but changes to "ki" when conjugated); ~たら means "when ~; if; after"; how to form: Verb (た form) + ら)]

- ぜひ *zehi*—certainly; without fail; please; definitely

- 食べてみてください *tabete mite kudasai*—please try to eat (*mitarashi dango*); you must try (*mitarashi dango*) [from 食べる (to eat); ~てみてください is used to express a demand, suggestion to someone to do something for the first time; how to form: Verb て-form + みてください]

「みたらし団子」日本に来たら、ぜひ食べてみて ください。

REVIEW

Now, review core vocabulary before trying to read the story in natural Japanese (no furigana or spaces) on the next page.

- 日本のストリートフード nihon no sutori-to fu-do—street food in Japan; Japanese street food

- みたらし団子 mitarashi dango—mitarashi dango; skewered rice dumplings in a sweet soy glaze

- 団子 dango—dango; dumpling (usually sweet)

- 歴史 rekishi—history

- 甘辛いたれ amakarai tare—sweet and salty sauce

- 丸い marui—round; circular

- 串にさして焼きます kushi ni sashite yakimasu—grilled on a skewer

- とてもおいしい totemo oishii—very delicious

- 祭り matsuri—festival

THE STORY
Now, let's read the story once more in natural Japanese.

今回は、「みたらし団子」をご紹介します
。

日本のストリートフードでとても長い歴史
があります。みたらし団子は、小さな丸い団子
です。4個から5個、串にさして焼きます。そ
れから、甘辛いたれをかけます。

とてもおいしいですよ。

みたらし団子は京都で始まりました。京都
のある祭りでみたらし団子がとても有名になり
ました。この祭りは平安時代からあります。み
たらし団子も千年以上の歴史があることになり
ます。

「みたらし団子」日本に来たら、ぜひ食べ
てみてください。

ENGLISH

Lastly, check the English translation to make sure you understand.

This time, we will introduce "Mitarashi Dango". It is a Japanese street food with a very long history.

Mitarashi dango are small round dumplings, consisting of four to five dumplings, grilled on a skewer. Then, they are topped with a sweet and spicy sauce. They are very delicious.

Mitarashi dango originated in Kyoto. Mitarashi dango became very famous at a festival in Kyoto. This festival has been around since the Heian period (794-1185). Mitarashi dango have a history of more than 1,000 years.

If you come to Japan, you must try "Mitarashi Dango".

Story 3 Japanese Pancakes

にほん
日本のパンケーキ

Normal Speed **Slow Speed**

https://commons.wikimedia.org/wiki/File:Pancakes,_%22S
mart_Coffee%22,_Ky%C5%8Dto.jpg

にほん　の　ぱんけーき　は、あめりか　の　ぱ
んけーき　と　ちょっと　ちがいます。

- 日本のパンケーキ nihon no panke-ki—Japanese pancake [日本の (Japanese; 日本 (Japan) + の (of; 's; modifier)) + パンケーキ (pancake)]

- は wa—(indicates the sentence topic)

- アメリカのパンケーキ amerika no panke-ki—American pancake [アメリカの (American; アメリカ (United States of America; United States; US; USA) + の ('s; of; modifier)) + パンケーキ (pancake)]

- と to—with; and; as [connecting particle]

- ちょっと chotto—somewhat; a bit; a little; slightly

- 違います chigaimasu—to differ (from); to be different; to be distinct

日本のパンケーキは、アメリカのパンケーキとちょっと違います。

とても　ふわふわ　で　やわらかい　です。

- とても totemo—very; awfully; exceedingly

- ふわふわでやわらかい fuwafuwa de yawarakai—fluffy and soft [ふわふわ (soft; fluffy; spongy) + で (て-form of です (be; is) which is used to connect to the next phrase, creating the meaning of "and") + やわらかい (soft; tender)]

- です desu—be; is

とてもふわふわでやわらかいです。

どうして　でしょう　か?　じつ　は、つくりか
た　が　ちがいます。

- どうして doushite—why; for what reason

- でしょうか deshou ka—(polite question marker)

- 実は jitsu wa—actually; as a matter of fact; in reality; fact is [実 (truth; reality) + は (adds emphasis)]

- 作り方が違います tsukurikata ga chigaimasu—the way to make (it) is different [作り方 (how to make) + が (emphasizes the preceding word; identifies what performs the action) + 違います (to differ (from); to be different; to be distinct)]

どうしてでしょうか?　実は、作り方が違います。

まず、たまご の しろみ を あわだてて め
れんげ を つくります。

- まず mazu—first (of all); firstly; to begin with

- たまごの白身 tamago no shiromi—whites of eggs; egg whites [たまご (eggs; egg; spawn; roe) + の (of; modifier) + 白身 (white meat; egg white)]

- を o—(indicates the direct object of action)

- 泡立てて awadatete—whip [て-form of 泡立てる (to beat (e.g. eggs); to whip (e.g. cream); to whisk) which is used to connect to the next phrase]

- メレンゲを作ります merenge o tsukurimasu—make meringue [メレンゲ (meringue) + を (indicates the direct object of action) + 作ります (ます/polite form of 作る (to make; to produce))]

まず、たまごの白身を泡立ててメレンゲを作り
ます。

これ に こむぎこ と たまご を いれて
まぜます。

- これに kore ni—in this; on this; hereto; to this [これ (this) + に (in; to; on)]

- 小麦粉とたまご komugiko to tamago—flour and eggs [小麦粉 (flour; wheat flour) + と (and) + たまご (egg)]

- 入れて混ぜます irete mazemasu—put and stir up [入れて (put and; て-form of 入れる (to put in; to let in) which is used to connect to the next verb 混ぜます) + 混ぜます (to mix; to stir; to blend)]

これに小麦粉とたまごを入れて混ぜます。

それ　から、そっと　ふらいぱん　に　いれて　やきます。

- それから sore kara—and then; after that; then

- そっと sotto—softly; gently; lightly

- フライパンに入れて焼きます furaipan ni irete yakimasu—put in a frying pan and bake (it) [フライパン (frying pan) + に (in) + 入れて (put and; て-form of 入れる (to put in; to let in) which is used to connect to the next verb 焼きます) + 焼きます (to bake; to roast; to toast)]

それから、そっとフライパンに入れて焼きます。

にほん　の　ぱんけーき　は、あめりか　の　ぱ
んけーき　の　に　ばい　くらい　の　たかさ
まで　ふくらみます。

- アメリカのパンケーキの2倍くらいの高さ amerika no panke-ki no ni bai kurai no takasa—about twice the height of American pancakes [アメリカの (American) + パンケーキ (pancake) + の (of; modifier) + 2倍 (double; twice (as much); twofold) + くらい (about; around; approximately) + 高さ (height; altitude)]

- まで made—to; up to

- 膨らみます fukuramimasu—to expand; to swell (out); to get big

日本のパンケーキは、アメリカのパンケーキの2倍くらいの高さまで膨らみます。

あなた　も　ぜひ　つくって　みて　ください。

- あなた anata—you

- も mo—too; also

- ぜひ zehi—certainly; without fail; please; definitely

- 作^{つく}ってみてください tsukutte mite kudasai—try making (it); please try to make (it) [from 作^{つく}る (to make; to prepare (food)); ~てみてください is used to express a demand, suggestion to someone to do something for the first time; how to form: Verb て-form + みてください]

あなたもぜひ作^{つく}ってみてください。

REVIEW

Now, review core vocabulary before trying to read the story in natural Japanese (no furigana or spaces) on the next page.

- 日本のパンケーキ *nihon no panke-ki*—Japanese pancake [日本の (Japanese; 日本 (Japan) + の (of; 's; modifier)) + パンケーキ (pancake)]

- アメリカのパンケーキ *amerika no panke-ki*—American pancake

- ふわふわでやわらかい *fuwafuwa de yawarakai*—fluffy and soft

- 違います *chigaimasu*—to differ (from)

- たまごの白身 *tamago no shiromi*—whites of eggs; egg whites

- メレンゲ *merenge*—meringue

- 小麦粉とたまご *komugiko to tamago*—flour and eggs

- フライパン *furaipan*—frying pan

- 膨らみます *fukuramimasu*—to expand; to swell (out); to get big

THE STORY

Now, let's read the story once more in natural Japanese.

　日本のパンケーキは、アメリカのパンケーキとちょっと違います。とてもふわふわでやわらかいです。どうしてでしょうか？

　実は、作り方が違います。まず、たまごの白身を泡立ててメレンゲを作ります。これに小麦粉とたまごを入れて混ぜます。それから、そっとフライパンに入れて焼きます。

　日本のパンケーキは、アメリカのパンケーキの２倍くらいの高さまで膨らみます。あなたもぜひ作ってみてください。

ENGLISH

Lastly, check the English translation to make sure you understand.

Japanese pancakes are somewhat different from American pancakes. They are very fluffy and soft. Why is that?

Actually, the way to make it is different. First, whip the whites of eggs to make meringue. Add flour and eggs to this mixture and stir it up. Then gently put it in a frying pan and bake it.

Japanese pancakes expand to about twice the height of American pancakes. You should try making them too.

Story 4 Japanese Dialects

にほん　　ほうげん
日本の方言

Normal Speed

Slow Speed

にほんご に は、ほうげん が あります。ち
ほう に よって、ことば が ぜんぜん ちが
う こと が あります。

- 日本語には nihongo ni wa—in the Japanese language
  [日本語 (Japanese (language)) + には (in; puts more
  emphasis and restriction on the preceding word 日本語)]

- 方言があります hougen ga arimasu—(Japanese language)
  has dialects [方言 (dialect; provincialism) + が (emphasizes
  the preceding word 方言) + あります (to have; to exist)]

- 地方によって chihou ni yotte—depending on the region
  [地方 (district; region; area) + によって (by; depending on)]

- 言葉が全然違う事があります kotoba ga zenzen chigau
  koto ga arimasu—the words can be totally different; there
  are times when the words are completely different [言葉
  (word; term; phrase; language) + が (emphasizes the
  preceding word 言葉) + 全然 (totally; entirely; completely)
  + 違う (to be different; to vary) + 事があります (there are
  times when; sometimes do ~)]

日本語には、方言があります。地方によって、
言葉が全然違う事があります。

あおもり けん の ほうげん を きいて も、
とうきょう の ひと は りかい し にくい
です。

- 青森県の方言を聞いても aomori ken no hougen o kiite mo—even if (you) listen to the dialect of Aomori Prefecture [青森県 (Aomori Prefecture) + の (of; modifier) + 方言 (dialect; provincialism) + を (indicates the direct object of action) + 聞いても (even if (you) listen; from 聞く (to listen; to hear); ~ても means "even if; even; even though ~"; how to form: Verb て-form + も)]

- 東京の人は toukyou no hito wa—people in Tokyo; Tokyo people [東京 (Tokyo) + の (of; in; modifier) + 人 (people) + は (indicates the sentence topic)]

- 理解しにくい rikai shi nikui—difficult to understand [from 理解する (understand; comprehend; grasp the details); ~にくい means "difficult to do ~"; how to form: Verb (ます-stem form) + にくい]

- です desu—be; is

青森県の方言を聞いても、東京の人は
理解しにくいです。

にほんご と は おもえない くらい はつお
ん や ことばづかい が ちがいます。

- 日本語とは思えない nihongo to wa omoenai—it is hard to believe it is Japanese; can hardly be expected to be Japanese [日本語 (Japanese (language)) + とは (indicates the word or phrase being defined) + 思えない (can't think; hard to believe; plain potential negative form of 思う (to think))]

- くらい kurai—so ... that ...; so (different) that (it is hard to believe it's Japanese)

- 発音や言葉づかい hatsuon ya kotoba zukai—pronunciation and wording [発音 (pronunciation) + や (and; connecting particle; how to form: Noun + や + Noun) + 言葉づかい (wording; speech; expression)]

- 発音や言葉づかいが違います hatsuon ya kotoba zukai ga chigaimasu—pronunciation and wording are different [発音や言葉づかい (pronunciation and wording) + が (subject of the phrase) + 違います (to be different; to vary)]

日本語とは思えないくらい発音や言葉づかいが
違います。

さいきん は、ほうげん を はなす わかい
ひと が すくなく なって きて います が、

- 最近は saikin wa—recently; nowadays [最近 (recently; nowadays; these days) + は (adds emphasis)]

- 方言を話す hougen o hanasu—speak dialects [方言 (dialect; provincialism) + を (indicates the direct object of action) + 話す (to speak; to talk; to converse)]

- 若い人が wakai hito ga—young people; youth [若い (young; youthful) + 人 (person; people) + が (emphasizes the preceding word)]

- 少なくなってきています sukunaku natte kite imasu—is decreasing; there are not many; started reducing [from 少なくなる (become fewer; drop away; shrink); 「~なってきています」 is the ています-form of 「~なってくる(start to; be getting; becoming to)」 which is used to describe a continuous action; how to form: Verb て-form + きています]

- が ga—but; however

最近は、方言を話す若い人が少なくなって
きていますが、

まだまだ　ほうげん　で　はなす　ひと　は　た
くさん　います。

- まだまだ madamada—still; much more

- 方言で hougen de—(speak) in dialects [方言 (dialect; provincialism) + で (in)]

- 話す人は hanasu hito wa—people who speak [話す (to speak; to converse) + 人 (people; person) + は (indicates the sentence topic)]

- たくさん takusan—many; a lot; a large number

- います imasu—there is/are (living things)

まだまだ方言で話す人はたくさんいます。

ほうげん　も　にほんご　です。

- 方言も日本語です hougen mo nihongo desu—dialects are also Japanese [方言 (dialect; provincialism) + も (also; too; as well) + 日本語 (Japanese (language)) + です (be; is)]

方言も日本語です。

おもしろい　ので、べんきょう　して　みて　く
ださい。

- おもしろい omoshiroi—interesting; fascinating

- ので node—so; that being the case; because of ...; the reason is ... [explains the reason for action]

- 勉強してみてください benkyou shite mite kudasai—please try to study (it) [from 勉強する (to study); ~てみてください is used to express a demand, suggestion to someone to do something for the first time; how to form: Verb て-form + みてください]

おもしろいので、勉強してみてください。

REVIEW

Now, review core vocabulary before trying to read the story in natural Japanese (no furigana or spaces) on the next page.

- 方言 *hougen*—dialect; provincialism

- 地方 *chihou*—district; region; area

- 言葉 *kotoba*—word; term; phrase; language

- 全然違う *zenzen chigau*—totally different; completely different [全然 (totally; completely) + 違う (to be different; to vary)]

- 青森県の方言 *aomori ken no hougen*—dialect of Aomori Prefecture

- 東京の人 *toukyou no hito*—people in Tokyo

- 理解しにくい *rikai shi nikui*—difficult to understand [from 理解する (to understand); ~にくい means "difficult to do ~"]

- 発音や言葉づかい *hatsuon ya kotoba zukai*—pronunciation and wording

- おもしろい *omoshiroi*—interesting; fascinating

- 勉強してみてください *benkyou shite mite kudasai*—please try to study (it) [from 勉強する (to study)]

- 発音や言葉づかい *hatsuon ya kotoba zukai*—pronunciation and wording

- おもしろい *omoshiroi*—interesting; fascinating

- 勉強してみてください *benkyou shite mite kudasai*—please try to study (it) [from 勉強する (to study)]

THE STORY

Now, let's read the story once more in natural Japanese.

　日本語には、方言があります。地方によって、言葉が全然違う事があります。青森県の方言を聞いても、東京の人は理解しにくいです。日本語とは思えないくらい発音や言葉づかいが違います。

　最近は、方言を話す若い人が少なくなってきていますが、まだまだ方言で話す人はたくさんいます。方言も日本語です。おもしろいので、勉強してみてください。

ENGLISH

Lastly, check the English translation to make sure you understand.

The Japanese language has dialects. Depending on the region, the words can be totally different. It is difficult for people in Tokyo to understand the dialect of Aomori Prefecture even if they listen to it. The pronunciation and wording are so different that it is hard to believe it is Japanese.

Recently, the number of young people who speak dialects is decreasing, but there are still many people who speak in dialects. These dialects are also Japanese. It is interesting, so please try to study it.

Story 5 Cold Meals

Normal Speed

Slow Speed

https://commons.wikimedia.org/wiki/File:Soumen1111.jpg

あめりか　や　よーろっぱ　で　は、つめたい
しょくじ　は　あまりたべません。

- アメリカやヨーロッパ amerika ya yo-roppa—United States and Europe [アメリカ (America; United States; US; USA) + や (and) + ヨーロッパ (Europe)]

- では de wa—in [で (in; at; indicates the location of action) + は (adds emphasis)]

- 冷たい食事 tsumetai shokuji—cold meals [冷たい (cold (to the touch); chilly; icy; freezing) + 食事 (meal)]

- は wa—(indicates the sentence topic)

- あまり食べません amari tabemasen—is/are not eaten very often; not eat very much [from 食べる (to eat); あまり~ない means "not very; not much ~"; how to form: あまり + Verb (negative form)]

アメリカやヨーロッパでは、冷たい食事はあま
り食べません。

つめたい　もの　は、　おいしくない　と　おも
われて　います。

- 冷たいもの tsumetai mono—cold food; cold meal [冷^{つめ}たい (cold) + もの (substance; thing)]

- おいしくない oishikunai—not tasty [plain negative form of おいしい (good(-tasting); nice; delicious; tasty)]

- と思われています to omowarete imasu—is/are considered [と (used for quoting (thoughts, speech, etc.)) + 思^{おも}われています (ています-form of 思^{おも}われる (plain passive form of 思^{おも}う (to think; to consider; to believe)) which is used to describe the actual state or condition of the subject)]

冷^{つめ}たいものは、おいしくないと思^{おも}われています。

でも、にほん　で　は　なつ　に　なる　と、う
どん　や　そば　などを

- でも demo—but; however

- 日本では nihon de wa—in Japan [日本 (Japan) + では (in)]

- 夏になると natsu ni naru to—in summer; with the arrival of summer; come summer [夏 (summer) + になると (when it becomes; when it comes to; になる (come to; become; turn out) + と (if; when))]

- うどんやそば udon ya soba—udon and soba [うどん (udon; thick Japanese wheat noodles) + や (and; such things as ...) + そば (soba; Japanese buckwheat noodles)]

- など nado—et cetera; etc.; and the like; and so forth

- を o—(indicates the direct object of action)

でも、日本では夏になると、うどんやそばなど
を

つめたく　して　たべます。

- 冷たくして食べます tsumetaku shite tabemasu—eat (it) cold; make (it) cold and eat [冷たくして (make it cold; て-form of 冷たくする (from 冷たい (cold (to the touch); chilly; icy); ～くする means "to make something whatever the adjective describes"; how to form: い-adjective い + くする) which is used to connect to the next verb) + 食べます (eat)]

冷たくして食べます。

にほん　の　なつ　は、とても　むしあつく、つ
めたい　もの　の　ほう　が　たべやすい　から
です。

- 日本の夏 nihon no natsu—summer in Japan [日本 (Japan) + の (of; 's; in; modifier) + 夏 (summer)]

- とても totemo—very

- 蒸し暑く mushiatsuku—hot and humid, and [adverbial form of 蒸し暑い (hot and humid; steaming hot; sultry) which is used to connect to the next phrase, creating the meaning of "and"]

- 冷たいもののほうが食べやすい tsumetai mono no hou ga tabeyasui—cold food is easier to eat [冷たい (cold (to the touch)) + もの (substance) + のほうが (conveys the idea that the noun it follows is "better" or "worse", "more" or "less", etc., depending on the sentence context) + 食べやすい (easy to eat; from 食べる (to eat); ~やすい means "easy to; likely to; prone to"; how to form: Verb (ます-stem form) + やすい)]

- からです kara—because; since

日本の夏は、とても蒸し暑く、冷たいもののほ
うが食べやすいからです。

つめたい　そうめん　など　は　とても　おいし
　　　　い　です　ね。

- 冷たいそうめん tsumetai soumen—cold soumen [冷<ruby>冷<rt>つめ</rt></ruby>たい (cold) + そうめん (soumen; fine white noodles)]

- とてもおいしい totemo oishii—taste very great; very tasty [とても (very; exceedingly) + おいしい (good(-tasting); nice; delicious; tasty)]

- ね ne—(sentence ender) [is used to express your opinion]

<ruby>冷<rt>つめ</rt></ruby>たいそうめんなどはとてもおいしいですね。

REVIEW

Now, review core vocabulary before trying to read the story in natural Japanese (no furigana or spaces) on the next page.

- 冷たい食事 *tsumetai shokuji*—cold meals [冷たい (cold (to the touch); chilly; freezing) + 食事 (meal)

- アメリカやヨーロッパ *amerika ya yo-roppa*—United States and Europe [アメリカ (America; USA) + や (and) + ヨーロッパ (Europe)]

- おいしくない *oishikunai*—not tasty

- 夏 *natsu*—summer

- うどんやそば *udon ya soba*—udon and *soba* [うどん (*udon*; thick Japanese wheat noodles) + や (and; such things as ...) + そば (*soba*; Japanese buckwheat noodles)]

- 蒸し暑い *mushiatsui*—hot and humid; steaming hot; sultry)

- 冷たいそうめん *tsumetai soumen*—cold *soumen* [冷たい (cold) + そうめん (*soumen*; fine white noodles)]

- とてもおいしい *totemo oishii*—taste very great; very tasty [とても (very; exceedingly) + おいしい (good(-tasting); nice; delicious; tasty)]

THE STORY

Now, let's read the story once more in natural Japanese.

アメリカやヨーロッパでは、冷たい食事はあまり食べません。冷たいものは、おいしくないと思われています。でも、日本では夏になると、うどんやそばなどを冷たくして食べます。

日本の夏は、とても蒸し暑く、冷たいもののほうが食べやすいからです。冷たいそうめんなどはとてもおいしいですね。

ENGLISH

In the United States and Europe, cold meals are not eaten very often. Cold foods are considered not tasty. However, in Japan, people eat udon and soba noodles cold in the summer.

This is because summer in Japan is very hot and humid, and cold food is easier to eat. Cold soumen noodles tastes very great.

Story 6 Disaster Preparedness Day

ぼうさい　ひ
防災の日

Normal Speed

Slow Speed

くがつ ついたち は「ぼうさい の ひ」で
す。ぼうさい の ひは、じしん や おおあめ
など の ため に ように を する ひ で
す。

- 9月1日 *ku gatsu tsuitachi*—September 1 [9月 (September; 月 (month)) + 1日 (1st day of the month)]

- は *wa*—(indicates the sentence topic)

- 「防災の日」 *「bousai no hi」* —"Disaster Preparedness Day" [「」 (quotation marks; " ") + 防災 (disaster preparedness; prevention of damage resulting from a natural disaster; protection against disaster) + の (of; modifier) + 日 (day)]

- です *desu*—be; is

- 地震や大雨などのために *jishin ya ooame nado no tame ni*—for earthquakes, heavy rain, etc. [地震 (earthquake) + や (such things as ...; and ... and) + 大雨 (heavy rain) + など (et cetera; etc.; and the like; and so forth) + のために (for)]

- 用意をする日です *youi o suru hi desu*—is a day to prepare [用意をする (get ready; prepare) + 日 (day) + です (be; is)]

9月1日は「防災の日」です。防災の日は、
地震や大雨などのために用意をする日です。

この　ひ　は、いろいろな　ばしょ　で　じしん　が　おこった　ときの　ため　の　くんれん　が　おこなわれます。

- この日は *kono hi wa*—this day [この (this) + 日 (day) + は (indicates the sentence topic)]

- いろいろな場所で *iroirona basho de*—in various places [いろいろな (various; all sorts of; variety of) + 場所 (place; location; spot) + で (at; in; indicates the location of action)]

- 地震が起こったときのための訓練が行われます *jishin ga okotta toki no tame no kunren ga okonawaremasu*—drills are held to prepare for earthquakes; drills are conducted for the time when earthquake occurred [地震 (earthquake) + が (indicates the subject of the verb) + 起こった (occurred; plain past form of 起こる (to occur; to happen)) + とき (time; moment) + のための (for;「Noun-A + のための + Noun-B」means that Noun-B is for the benefit of Noun-A) + 訓練 (training; drill; practice) + が (identifies what performs the action; emphasizes the preceding word) + 行われます (is/are held; polite passive positive form of 行う (hold; conduct; perform))]

この日は、いろいろな場所で地震が起こったときのための訓練が行われます。

せんきゅうひゃくにじゅうさん　ねん（たいしょ
う　じゅうに　ねん）く　がつ　ついたち　に
かんとう　だいしんさい　が　おこりました。

- 1923年（大正12年）9月1日に *sen kyuu hyaku ni juu san nen (taishou juu ni nen) ku gatsu tsuitachi ni*—on September 1, 1923 (Taishou 12) [1923年 (1923; 年 (year)) + 大正12年 (Taishou 12; 大正 (Taishou)) + 9月1日 (September 1) + に (on; specifies time)]

- 関東大震災が起こりました *kantou daishinsai ga okorimashita*—the Great Kanto earthquake occurred [関東 (Kantou; region consisting of Tokyo and surrounding prefectures) + 大震災 (great earthquake (disaster)) + が (identifies what performs the action; emphasizes the preceding word) + 起こりました (occurred; polite past form of 起こる (to occur; to happen))]

1923年（大正12年）9月1日に関東大震災が起こりました。

この ひ を わすれない よう に と いう
いみ で、く がつ ついたち が 「ぼうさい
の ひ」に なりました。

- この日を忘れないように *kono hi o wasurenai you ni*—to remember this day; so that (you) won't forget this day [この (this) + 日 (day) + を (indicates the direct object of action) + 忘れないように (so that ... won't forget; 忘れない (don't forget; plain negative form of 忘れる (to forget)) + ように (so that ~; in order to); how to form: Verb (ない-form) + ように)]

- という意味で *to iu imi de*—mean; that means [という (that) + 意味 (meaning; significance; sense) + で (て-form of です (be; is) which is used to connect to the next phrase)]

- 9月1日が「防災の日」になりました *ku gatsu tsuitachi ga「bousai no hi」ni narimashita*—September 1 became the "Disaster Preparedness Day" [9月1日 (September 1) + が (emphasizes the preceding word) + 「防災の日」 ("Disaster Preparedness Day") + になりました (became; polite past form of になる (become; turn out; come to))]

この日を忘れないようにという意味で、9月
1日が「防災の日」になりました。

にほん は、じしん や たいふう など さい
がい の おおい くに です。

- 日本は *nihon wa*—Japan [日本 (Japan) + は (indicates the sentence topic)]

- 地震や台風など *jishin ya taifuu nado*—such as earthquakes and typhoons [地震 (earthquake) + や (such things as ...; and) + 台風 (typhoon; hurricane) + など (et cetera; etc.; and the like; and so forth)]

- 災害の多い国です *saigai no ooi kuni desu*—is a country prone to disasters [災害 (calamity; disaster) + の (of; modifier) + 多い (frequent; common; a lot; many; prone) + 国 (country; state) + です (be; is)]

日本は、地震や台風など災害の多い国です。

ひごろ　から　じゅんび　を　して　おきましょ
う。

- 日ごろから *higoro kara*—on a regular basis; on a daily basis; on a routine basis [日ごろ (normally; habitually) + から (from; by; on)]

- 準備をしておきましょう *junbi o shite okimashou*—be prepared; let's get ready in advance [from 準備をする (get ready; make preparations); ～ておきましょう is the polite volitional form of ～ておく (to do something in advance; how to form: Verb て-form + おく); volitional form is used when making a suggestion to one or more people including oneself]

日ごろから準備をしておきましょう。

REVIEW

Now, review core vocabulary before trying to read the story in natural Japanese (no furigana or spaces).

- 9月1日 *ku gatsu tsuitachi*—September 1 [9月 (September) + 1日 (1st day of the month)]

- 関東大震災 *kantou daishinsai*—Great Kanto earthquake of 1923

- 防災の日 *bousai no hi*—Disaster Preparedness Day

- 地震 *jishin*—earthquake

- 大雨 *ooame*—heavy rain

- 台風 *taifuu*—typhoon; hurricane

- 災害 *saigai*—calamity; disaster

- 訓練 *kunren*—training; drill; practice

- 日ごろ *higoro*—normally; habitually

- 準備をしておきましょう *junbi o shite okimashou*—be prepared; let's get ready in advance

- 用意をする *youi o suru*—get ready; prepare

THE STORY

Now, let's read the story once more in natural Japanese.

9月1日は「防災の日」です。防災の日は、地震や大雨などのために用意をする日です。この日は、いろいろな場所で地震が起こったときのための訓練が行われます。

1923年（大正12年）9月1日に関東大震災が起こりました。この日を忘れないようにという意味で、9月1日が「防災の日」になりました。日本は、地震や台風など災害の多い国です。日ごろから準備をしておきましょう。

ENGLISH

September 1 is "Disaster Preparedness Day". Disaster Preparedness Day is a day to prepare for earthquakes and heavy rain. On this day, drills are held in various places to prepare for earthquakes.

1923 (Taishou 12), on September 1, the Great Kanto earthquake occurred. September 1 was designated as "Disaster Preparedness Day" to remember this day. Japan is a country prone to disasters such as earthquakes and typhoons. Be prepared on a daily basis.

Story 7 Sports Day

スポーツの日

Normal Speed

Slow Speed

じゅう　がつ　に　は、「スポーツ　の　ひ」と
いう　しゅくじつ　が　あります。

10月には juu gatsu ni wa—in October [10月 (October) + には (in; puts more emphasis and restriction on the preceding word)]

「スポーツの日」 「supo-tsu no hi」 —"Sports Day" [「」 (quotation marks; " ") + スポーツ (sport; sports) + の ('s; of; modifier) + 日 (day)]

「スポーツの日」という 祝 日 「supo-tsu no hi」 to iu shukujitsu—a national holiday called "Sports Day" [「スポーツの日」 ("Sports Day") + という (called; named) + 祝 日 (national holiday; public holiday)]

(が)あります (ga) arimasu—there is/are (non-living things)

１０月には、「スポーツの日」という 祝 日 が
あります。

もともと　は、「たいいく　の　ひ」と　よばれ
る　しゅくじつ　でした。

- もともとは motomoto wa—originally [もともと (originally; from the start; from the beginning; by nature) + は (adds emphasis)]

- 「体育の日」「taiiku no hi」—"Health-Sports Day" [「」 (quotation marks; " ") + 体育 (physical education; Health-Sports) + の ('s; of) + 日 (day)]

- 「体育の日」と呼ばれる祝日でした 「taiiku no hi」to yobareru shukujitsu deshita—the national holiday was called "Health-Sports Day" [「体育の日」("Health-Sports Day") + と (quotation marker) + 呼ばれる (to be called (a name); to be referred to (as); plain passive positive form of 呼ぶ (to call; to designate)) + 祝日 (national holiday; public holiday) + でした (was/were; plain past form です (be; is))]

もともとは、「体育の日」と呼ばれる祝日でした。

せんきゅうひゃくろくじゅうよ　ねん　じゅう
がつ　とおか　に　にほん　で　はじめて　の
とうきょう　オリンピック　が　おこなわれまし
た。

- 1964年10月１０日に sen kyuu hyaku roku juu yo nen juu gatsu tooka ni—on October 10, 1964 [1964年 (1964; 年 (year)) + １０月１０日 (October 10) + に (in; on; specifies time)]

- 日本で nihon de—in Japan [日本 (Japan) + で (in; indicates the location of action)]

- 初めての東京オリンピックが行われました hajimete no toukyou orinpikku ga okonawaremashita—the first Tokyo Olympics were held (in Japan) [初めて (for the first time; first) + の (of; modifier) + 東京 (Tokyo) + オリンピック (Olympics; Olympic Games) + が (identifies what performs the action; emphasizes the preceding word) + 行われました (was/were held; polite past form of 行われる (plain passive positive form of 行う (to hold; to conduct; to perform)))]

１９６４年10月１０日に日本で初めての東京オリンピックが行われました。

これ を きねん して じゅう がつ とおか が たいいく の ひ に なりました。

- これを記念して kore o kinen shite—to commemorate this (event) [これ (this) + を (indicates the direct object of action) + 記念して (commemorate; て-form of 記念する (to celebrate; to commemorate))]

- 10月10日が体育の日になりました juu gatsu tooka ga taiiku no hi ni narimashita—October 10 became Health-Sports Day [10月10日 (October 10) + が (emphasizes the preceding word) + 体育の日 (Health-Sports Day) + になりました (became; polite past form of になる (become; come to; turn to))]

これを記念して１０月10日が体育の日になりました。

れいわ に ねん から は、じゅう がつ の
だい に げつようび が「スポーツ の ひ」
に なりました。

- 令和2年からは reiwa ni nen kara wa—from 2020 [令和2年 (2020; 令和 (Reiwa era (May 1, 2019-))) + から (from; since) + は (adds emphasis)]

- 10月の第2月曜日が juu gatsu no dai ni getsuyoubi ga—the second Monday of October [１０月 (October) + の (of; modifier) + 第2 (second) + 月曜日 (Monday) + が (emphasizes the preceding word; identifies what performs the action)]

- 「スポーツの日」になりました 「supo-tsu no hi」 ni narimashita—became "Sports Day" [「スポーツの日」 ("Sports Day") + になりました (became; polite past form of になる (become; come to; turn to))]

令和2年からは、１０月の第2月曜日が「スポーツの日」になりました。

ことし の スポーツ の ひ は、じゅう が
つ とおか (げつ) です。

- 今年のスポーツの日は kotoshi no supo-tsu no hi wa—the
  Sports Day of this year [今年 (this year) + の (of; modifier) + ス
  ポーツの日 (Sports Day) + は (indicates the sentence topic);
  this was written in 2022, so "this year" refers to October 2022]

- 10月10日 (月) です juu gatsu tooka (getsu) desu—is
  Monday, October 10 [１０月10日 (October 10) + 月 (short for
  "Monday" (月曜日)) + です (be; is)]

今年のスポーツの日は、１０月10日 (月) で
す。

REVIEW

Now, review core vocabulary before trying to read the story in natural Japanese (no furigana or spaces).

- スポーツの日 *supo-tsu no hi*—sports day [スポーツ (sport; sports) + の ('s; of; modifier) + 日 (day)]

- 体育の日 *taiiku no hi*—health-sports day [体育 (physical education; health-sports) + の ('s; of) + 日 (day)]

- 祝日 *shukujitsu*—national holiday

- 東京オリンピック *toukyou orinpikku*—Tokyo Olympics [東京 (Tokyo) + オリンピック (Olympics; Olympic Games)]

- 記念 *kinen*—commemoration; celebration; memory

- 10月10日 *juu gatsu tooka*—October 10 [10月 (October) + 10日 (10th day of the month)]

- 月曜日 *getsuyoubi*—Monday

- 令和 *reiwa*—Reiwa era (May 1, 2019-)

- もともと *motomoto*—originally; from the start

THE STORY

Now, let's read the story once more in natural Japanese.

10月には、「スポーツの日」という祝日があります。もともとは、「体育の日」と呼ばれる祝日でした。1964年10月１０日に日本で初めての東京オリンピックが行われました。これを記念して10月10日が体育の日になりました。令和2年からは、10月の第2月曜日が「スポーツの日」になりました。今年のスポーツの日は、10月10日（月）です。

ENGLISH

In October, there is a national holiday called "Sports Day". Originally, the national holiday was called "Health-Sports Day". On October 10, 1964, the first Tokyo Olympics were held in Japan. To commemorate this event, October 10 became Health-Sports Day. Since 2020, the second Monday of October has become "Sports Day". This year's Sports Day is Monday, October 10.

Story 8 Japanese Names

<ruby>日本人<rt>にほんじん</rt></ruby>の<ruby>名前<rt>なまえ</rt></ruby>

Normal Speed　　　**Slow Speed**

にほんじん　の　なまえ　は　すごく　むずかし
い　です。でも　にほんご　が　うまく　なりた
い　なら、

- 日本人の名前 nihonjin no namae—Japanese names [日本人
  (Japanese; Japanese national; the people of Japan) + の (of; 's;
  modification) + 名前 (name)]

- は wa—(indicates the sentence topic)

- すごく 難しい sugoku muzukashii—very difficult [すごく
  (awfully; very; immensely) + 難しい (difficult; hard;
  complicated)]

- です desu—be; is

- でも demo—but; however

- 日本語がうまくなりたいなら nihongo ga umaku naritai
  nara—if (you) want to be good at Japanese [日本語 (Japanese
  (language)) + が (emphasizes the preceding word) + うまく
  (good; skillfully; proficiently; successfully) + なりたい (want to
  be; want to become; from なる (to become; to get; to turn; to
  reach; to attain); ~たい means "want to do something"; how to
  use: Verb (ます-stem form) + たい) + なら (if; in case)]

日本人の名前はすごく 難しいです。でも日本語
がうまくなりたいなら、

ほんじん の なまえ を よめる よう に
なった ほう が いい でしょう。

- 日本人の名前を読めるようになったほうがいい nihonjin no namae o yomeru you ni natta hou ga ii—(you) should learn to read Japanese names [日本人の名前 (Japanese names) + を (indicates the direct object of action) + 読める (can read; plain potential positive form of 読む (to read)) + ようになった (came to be that; turned into ~; reached the point that) + ほうがいい (should ~; it'd be better to)]

- でしょう deshou—I think; it seems; right?; don't you agree?; I guess

日本人の名前を読めるようになったほうがいいでしょう。

ある　あめりかじん　は、にほん　の　ちゅうが
っこう　で　えいご　を　おしえて　いました。

- あるアメリカ人は aru amerikajin wa—an American; an American person [ある (a certain; some) + アメリカ人 (American; アメリカ (America; United States; US; USA) + 人 (person; -ian (e.g. Italian); -ite (Tokyoite))) + は (indicates the sentence topic)]

- 日本の中学校で nihon no chuugakkou de—at a Japanese junior high school [日本 (Japan) + の (of; 's; modifier) + 中学校 (junior high school; middle school; lower secondary school) + で (at; in)]

- 英語を教えていました eigo o oshiete imashita—was teaching English [英語 (English (language)) + を (indicates the direct object of action) + 教えていました (was teaching; ていました form of 教える (to teach; to instruct) which is used to describe an ongoing action happening in the past; how to form: Verb て-form + いました)]

あるアメリカ人は、日本の中学校で英語を教
えていました。

がんばって　がくせい　の　なまえ　を　ぜんい
ん　おぼえよう　と　しました　が、

- がんばって ganbatte—do your best; go for it; hang in there; keep at it; try your best

- 学生の名前を全員覚えようとしました gakusei no namae o zenin oboeyou to shimashita—tried to remember all the student's names [学生 (student (especially a university student)) + の ('s; of; modifier) + 名前 (name) + を (indicates the direct object of action) + 全員 (all; everyone; everybody; all members) + 覚えようとしました (tried to remember; from 覚える (to remember; to memorize; to bear in mind); ~ようとしました is the polite past form of ~ようとする (try to; attempt to); how to form: Verb (volitional form) + としました)]

- が ga—but; however

がんばって学生の名前を全員覚えようとしま
したが、

にほんじん　の　なまえ　を　おぼえる　の　は
とても　たいへん　でした。

- 日本人の名前を覚えるのは nihonjin no namae o oboeru no wa—to remember Japanese names [日本人の名前 (Japanese names) + を (indicates the direct object of action) + 覚える (to remember; to memorize) + の (nominalizer; turns the preceding clause into a noun phrase) + は (indicates the sentence topic)]

- とても大変でした totemo taihen deshita—was very difficult [とても (very; awfully; exceedingly) + 大変 (difficult; hard; challenging) + でした (was; polite past form of です (be; is))]

日本人の名前を覚えるのはとても大変でした。

ある　くらす　に「にった」と　いう　なまえ
　　　の　せいと　が　いました。

- あるクラスに aru kurasu ni—in a certain class [ある (a certain; some) + クラス (class) + に (in)]

- 「新田」という名前の生徒がいました 「nitta」to iu namae no seito ga imashita—there was a student named 「新田」 [「新田」 (Nitta) + という (named; called) + 名前 (name) + の (of; modifier) + 生徒 (pupil; student; schoolchild) + が (identifies who performs the action) + いました (there was; polite past form of いる (to be (of animate objects); to exist))]

あるクラスに「新田」という名前の生徒がいました。

「あたらしい　たんぼ」と　かきます。

- 「新しい田んぼ」「atarashii tanbo」—"new rice field" [「」 (quotation marks; " ") + 新しい (new; latest; modern) + 田んぼ (rice field; paddy field; farm)]

- 「新しい田んぼ」と書きます「atarashii tanbo」to kakimasu—(it) is written as 「新しい田んぼ (new rice field)」 [「新しい田んぼ」 ("new rice field") + と (as; quotation marker) + 書きます (to write)]

「新しい田んぼ」と書きます。

その　あめりかじん　は　その　せいと　の　な
まえ　を　じしん　たっぷり　に　おおごえ　で
いいました。「しんだ　さん！」

- そのアメリカ人は sono amerikajin wa—the American (teacher) [その (the; that) + アメリカ人 (American person) + は (indicates the sentence topic)]

- その生徒の名前を自信たっぷりに大声で言いました sono seito no namae o jishin tappuri ni oogoe de iimashita—confidently and loudly said the student's name [その (the; that) + 生徒 (pupil; student; schoolchild) + の ('s; of; modifier) + 名前 (name) + を (indicates the direct object of action) + 自信たっぷりに (confidently; assertively; with a lot of confidence; the に is added to turn 自信たっぷり (confident; full of confidence) into an adverbial phrase) + 大声で (loudly; 大声 (loud voice) + で (in; with)) + 言いました (said; polite past form of 言う (to say; to utter))]

- 「しんださん！」「shinda san!」—"Shinda-san!" [「」 (quotation marks; " ") + しんださん (Shinda-san; さん is an honorific suffix which means Mr., Mrs., or Miss that can be used with both first and last names and both genders)]

そのアメリカ人はその生徒の名前を自信たっぷ
りに大声で言いました。「しんださん！」

せいとたち　は　みんな、おおわらい　しました。
「新田」は「にった」と　よみます。

- 生徒たちは 皆 seitotachi wa minna—all the students [生徒たち (students; たち is a pluralizing suffix (especially for people and animals)) + は (indicates the sentence topic; adds emphasis) + 皆 (all; everyone; everybody)]

- 大笑いしました oowarai shimashita—burst out laughing; laughed aloud [polite past form of 大笑いする (laugh aloud; have a great big laugh; burst out laughing)]

- 「新田」は「にった」と読みます 「nitta」 wa 「nitta」 to yomimasu—「新田」 is read as "Nitta" [「新田」 ("Nitta") + は (indicates the sentence topic) + 「にった」 ("Nitta") + と (as; quotation marker) + 読みます (to read)]

生徒たちは 皆 、大笑いしました。「新田」は「にった」と読みます。

「しんだ」は「Dead」と いう いみ が あ る ので、せいとたち は おおわらい した の です。

- 「しんだ」は「Dead」という意味がある「shinda」wa 「Dead」to iu imi ga aru—"Shinda" means "Dead" [「しんだ」("Shinda") + は (indicates the sentence topic) + 「Dead」("Dead") + という (that says; that; is used to define, describe, and generally just talk about the thing itself) + 意味がある (means; 意味 (meaning; significance; sense) + が (identifies what performs the action) + ある (to have; to be; to exist))]

- ので node—because; the reason is …

- 生徒たちは大笑いした seitotachi wa oowarai shita—the students laughed out loud [生徒たち (students; たち is a pluralizing suffix) + は (indicates the sentence topic) + 大笑いした (laughed aloud; plain past form of 大笑いする (laugh aloud; have a great big laugh; burst out laughing))]

- のです no desu—it is assuredly that …; can say with confidence that … [shows emphasis; to explain something]

「しんだ」は「Dead」という意味があるので、 生徒たちは大笑いしたのです。

REVIEW

Now, review core vocabulary before trying to read the story in natural Japanese (no furigana or spaces).

- 日本人 *nihonjin*—Japanese; the people of Japan

- アメリカ人 *amerikajin*—American person

- 名前 *namae*—name

- クラス *kurasu*—class

- 中学校 *chuugakkou*—junior high school

- がんばって *ganbatte*—do your best

- 覚える *oboeru*—to remember; to memorize

- 大変 *taihen*—difficult; hard; challenging

- 生徒 *seito*—pupil; student; schoolchild

- 学生 *gakusei*—student (especially a university student)

- 大笑い *oowarai*—great laughter; burst of laughter

THE STORY

Now, let's read the story once more in natural Japanese.

日本人の名前はすごく難しいです。でも日本語がうまくなりたいなら、日本人の名前を読めるようになったほうがいいでしょう。

あるアメリカ人は、日本の中学校で英語を教えていました。がんばって学生の名前を全員覚えようとしましたが、日本人の名前を覚えるのはとても大変でした。

あるクラスに「新田」という名前の生徒がいました。「新しい田んぼ」と書きます。そのアメリカ人はその生徒の名前を自信たっぷりに大声で言いました。「しんださん！」

生徒たちは皆、大笑いしました。「新田」は「にった」と読みます。「しんだ」は「Dead」という意味があるので、生徒たちは大笑いしたのです。

English

Japanese names are very difficult. But if you want to be good at Japanese, you should learn to read Japanese names.

An American was teaching English at a Japanese junior high school. He tried his best to remember all the students' names, but it was very difficult to remember Japanese names.

There was a student in one of his classes named 「新田」.It is written as 「新しい田んぼ (new rice field)」.

The American teacher confidently and loudly said the student's name: "Shinda-san!"

All the students burst out laughing.

The name 「新田」 is read as "Nitta". The students laughed out loud because "Shinda" means "Dead".

Story 9 General Cleaning

<ruby>大掃除<rt>おおそうじ</rt></ruby>

Normal Speed	Slow Speed

にほん　で　は、いち　ねん　の　おわり　に
おおそうじ　を　します。

- 大掃除 oosouji—major cleanup; spring cleaning; general cleaning; housecleaning

- 日本では nihon de wa—in Japan [日本 (Japan) + で (in; indicates the location of action) + は (adds emphasis)]

- 一年の終わりに ichi nen no owari ni—at the end of the year [一年 (one year; the year; 一 (one; 1) + 年 (year)) + の (of; modifier) + 終わり (end; ending; close) + に (at; specifies time)]

- 大掃除をします oosouji o shimasu—do a general cleaning; do housecleaning

日本では、一年の終わりに大掃除をします。

これ は、いち ねん の よごれ を とって、
あたらしい とし を むかえる ため の じ
ゅんび です。

- これは kore wa—this [これ (this; this one) + は (adds emphasis)]

- 一年の汚れを取って ichi nen no yogore o totte—remove the dirt of the year and [一年 (one year; the year) + の (of; modifier) + 汚れ (dirt; filth; stain) + を (indicates the direct object of action) + 取って (remove and; て-form of 取る (to remove; to get rid of; to take off) which is used to connect to the next phrase, creating the meaning of "and")]

- 新しい年を迎える atarashii toshi o mukaeru—to welcome the new year [新しい (new; recent; fresh) + 年 (year) + を (indicates the direct object of action) + 迎える (to receive; to welcome; to greet)]

- ための準備 tame no junbi—preparation for [ため (for) + の (modifier) + 準備 (preparation; arrangements; getting ready)]

- です desu—be; is

これは、一年の汚れを取って、新しい年を迎
えるための準備です。

じぶん　の　いえ　は　もちろん、がっこう　や
かいしゃ　で　も　そうじ　します。

- 自分の家はもちろん学校や会社でも jibun no ie wa mochiron gakkou ya kaisha de mo—not only at (their) own house but also at school and workplace [自分 (yourself; oneself; myself) + の (of; 's; indicates possessive) + 家 (house; residence; dwelling) + はもちろん (not only … but also ~; not to mention; let alone; of course; naturally; how to use: Noun + は もちろん + 2nd clause + も) + 学校 (school) + や (and) + 会社 (workplace; company; corporation) + で (at; indicates the location of action) + も (too; also; as well)]

- 掃除します souji shimasu—clean; tidy-up

自分の家はもちろん、学校や会社でも掃除します。

じゅうに　がつ　じゅうさん　にち　に　そうじ
をする　ちほう　が　おおい　の　です　が、

- １２月１３日に juu ni gatsu juu san nichi ni—on December 13 [１２月 (December) + １３日 (13th day of the month) + に (on; specifies time)]

- 掃除をする地方が多いのです souji o suru chihou ga ooi no desu—(in) many regions, (people) clean (on December 13) [掃除をする (clean; tidy-up; make a sweep; do the cleaning) + 地方 (district; region; area; locality) + が (emphasizes the preceding word) + 多い (many; numerous; a lot) + のです (to explain something; shows emphasis)]

- が ga—and (conjunction) [is used to combine two sentences together into one compound sentence]

１２月１３日に掃除をする地方が多いのですが、

これ　は、えど　じだい　に　しょうぐん　の
すんで　いた　えどじょう　で、

- これは kore wa—as for this [これ (this) + は (adds emphasis)]
- 江戸時代に edo jidai ni—in the Edo period [江戸 (Edo (shogunate capital, now Tokyo); Yedo) + 時代 (period; epoch; era; age) + に (in)]
- 将軍の住んでいた江戸城で shougun no sunde ita edojou de—in the Edo castle where the shogun lived [将軍 (general; shogun) + の (of; modifier) + 住んでいた (lived; ~ていた form of 住む (to live (of humans); to reside; to inhabit; to dwell) which places focus on the duration of a past action; how to form: Verb て-form + いた) + 江戸 (Edo (shogunate capital, now Tokyo)) + 城 (castle) + で (in; indicates the location of action)]

これは、江戸時代に将軍の住んでいた江戸城
で、

じゅうに　がつ　じゅうさん　にち　に　おおそ
うじ　を　して　いた　から　だ　そう　で
す。

- １２月１３日に大掃除をしていた juu ni gatsu juu san nichi ni oosouji o shite ita—used to have a general cleaning on December 13 [１２月 (December) + １３日 (13th day of the month) + に (on) + 大掃除をしていた (used to have a general cleaning; ~ていた form of 大掃除をする (do a major housecleaning; have a general cleaning) which places focus on the duration of a past action)]

- から kara—because; since

- だそうです da sou desu—I heard that; it is said that; it seems that [expresses what something appears to be based on what one heard from other people]

１２月１３日に大掃除をしていたからだそうです。

REVIEW

Now, review core vocabulary before trying to read the story
in natural Japanese (no furigana or spaces).

- 大掃除 *oosouji*—major cleanup; general cleaning

- 終わり *owari*—end; ending; close

- 汚れ *yogore*—dirt; filth; stain

- 新しい年 *atarashii toshi*—new year [新しい (new;
recent; fresh) + 年 (year)]

- 準備 *junbi*—preparation; getting ready

- 家 *ie*—house; residence; dwelling

- 学校 *gakkou*—school

- 会社 *kaisha*—workplace; company; corporation

- 地方 *chihou*—district; region; area; locality

- 多い *ooi*—many; numerous; a lot

- 江戸時代 *edo jidai*—Edo period (1603-1868)

- 江戸城 *edojou*—Edo castle

The Story

Now, let's read the story once more in natural Japanese.

日本では、一年の終わりに大掃除をします。これは、一年の汚れを取って、新しい年を迎えるための準備です。自分の家はもちろん、学校や会社でも掃除します。

12月13日に掃除をする地方が多いのですが、これは、江戸時代に将軍の住んでいた江戸城で、12月13日に大掃除をしていたからだそうです。

English

In Japan, they do a general cleaning at the end of the year. This is to remove the dirtiness of the year and prepare to welcome the new year. They clean not only their own house but also at school and workplace.

In many regions, people clean on December 13, because in the Edo period, the Edo castle where the shogun lived, used to have a general cleaning day on December 13.

Story 10 Motivation

モチベーション

Normal Speed

Slow Speed

もちべーしょん　は　とても　たいせつ　です。
くれい　さん　が　にほんご　を　べんきょう
し　はじめた　ばかり　の　ころ、

- モチベーションは mochibe-shon wa—motivation [モチベーション (motivation) + は (indicates the sentence topic)]

- とても大切 totemo taisetsu—very important

- クレイさんが kurei san ga—Clay [クレイさん (Clay; さん is an honorific suffix) + が (identifies who performs the action; emphasizes the preceding word)]

- 日本語を勉強し始めたばかりの頃 nihongo o benkyou shi hajimeta bakari no koro—when (Clay) first started studying Japanese [日本語 (Japanese (language)) + を (indicates the direct object of action) + 勉強し始めた (started studying; from 勉強する (to study); ~始めた is the plain past form of ~始める (to start; to begin to ~; is used in conjunction with another verb to indicate the beginning of "V (action)"); how to form: Verb ます (stem form) + 始めた) + ばかり (just (did something)) + の頃 (when; around; about; how to form: Noun + の + 頃)]

モチベーションはとても大切です。クレイさんが日本語を勉強し始めたばかりの頃、

「あたらしい」と いう ことば を おぼえました。

- 「新しい」という言葉を覚えました 「atarashii」to iu kotoba o oboemashita—(he) learned the word 「新しい」[「新しい」(" 新しい (new)"; 「」 (quotation marks; " ")) + という (called; that; is used to define, describe, and generally just talk about the thing itself) + 言葉 (word; phrase; expression; term) + を (indicates the direct object of action) + 覚えました (learned; polite past form of 覚える (to learn; to memorize; to remember))]

「新しい」という言葉を覚えました。

じしょ を みる と、「あたらしい」の まえ に あった の が「あざらし ((the animal) seal)」と いう ことば でした。

- 辞書を見ると jisho o miru to—when (he) looked in the dictionary [辞書 (dictionary) + を (direct object) + 見る (to see; to look) + と (when; if)

- 「新しい」の前にあったのが 「atarashii」no mae ni atta no ga—the (word) 「新しい」 was preceded by the (word); the (word) located before 「新しい」 [("新しい (new)") + の (of; tells the location) + 前 (before; in front; previous) + に (in; expresses the location) + あった (located; plain past form of ある (to be located; to have; to exist)) + の (a particle that acts like a noun; placeholder for nouns) + が (emphasizes the preceding word)]

- 「アザラシ (the animal seal)」という言葉 「azarashi (the animal seal)」to iu kotoba—the word "アザラシ" [「アザラシ (the animal seal)」 ("アザラシ (the animal seal)") + という (called; is used to define, describe, and generally just talk about the thing itself) + 言葉 (word; phrase; term)]

- でした deshita—was; were [polite past from of です (be; is)]

辞書を見ると、「新しい」の前にあったのが 「アザラシ (seal)」という言葉でした。

そこで、これ を おぼえる こと に しました。

- そこで sokode—so; accordingly; now; then; thereupon; therefore

- これを覚えることにしました kore o oboeru koto ni shimashita—(he) decided to learn it [これ (this; it) + を (indicates the direct object of action) + 覚える (to learn; to acquire; to memorize) + ことにしました (decided to; expresses one's decision to do something; how to form: Verb (dictionary form) + ことにしました)]

そこで、これを覚えることにしました。

「あたらしい あざらし」と なんど も いい ながら、ふたつ の たんご を おぼえました。

- 「新しいアザラシ」と何度も言いながら 「atarashii azarashi」 to nando mo iinagara—by saying 「新しいアザラシ」 over and over again [「新しいアザラシ」("新しいアザラシ (new-(the animal) seal)") + と (quotation marker; used for quoting speech) + 何度も (all too often; time and time again; over and over again; constantly) + 言いながら (by saying; while saying; from 言う (to say; to utter); ~ながら is a conjunction that joins two clauses together into one sentence and it can indicate two simultaneous actions, similar to "while" in English; how to form: Verb (ます-stem form) + ながら)]

- 2つの単語を覚えました futatsu no tango o oboemashita—learned the two words [2つ (two) + の (of; modifier) + 単語 (word; vocabulary) + を (indicates the direct object of action) + 覚えました (learned; polite past form of 覚える (to learn; to acquire; to memorize))]

「新しいアザラシ」と何度も言いながら、2つ の単語を覚えました。

「あたらしい」と「あざらし」の　ふたつ　です。

- 「新しい」と「アザラシ」の２つ 「atarashii」to
「azarashi」no futatsu—the two (words) 「新しい」and
「アザラシ」[「新しい」(" 新しい (new)") + と (and) +
「アザラシ」("アザラシ (seal (animal))") + の (of; modifier) +
２つ (two)]

「新しい」と「アザラシ」の２つです。

「あざらし」と いう ことば は にちじょう かいわ で は あまり つかわない かもしれ ません が、

- 「アザラシ」という言葉は 「azarashi」to iu kotoba wa—the word 「アザラシ」[「アザラシ」("アザラシ (seal (animal))") + という (called; is used to define, describe, and generally just talk about the thing itself) + 言葉 (word; phrase; term) + は (indicates the sentence topic)]

- 日常会話では nichijou kaiwa de wa—in everyday conversation [日常会話 (everyday conversation; day-to-day conversation) + で (in) + は (adds emphasis)]

- あまり amari—(not) very; (not) much

- 使わないかもしれません tsukawanai kamoshiremasen—may not be used [使わない (don't use; plain negative form of 使う (to use (a tool, method, etc.))) + かもしれません (might; perhaps; indicates possibility)]

- が ga—but; however

「アザラシ」という言葉は日常会話ではあまり 使わないかもしれませんが、

くれい さん は おもしろい ことば だ と
おもいました。

- 面白い言葉だと思いました omoshiroi kotoba da to omoimashita—(Clay) thought it was an interesting word [面白い (interesting; fascinating; intriguing; enthralling) + 言葉 (word; phrase; expression; term) + だと思いました (thought; this can be used to describe your own thoughts or someone else's thoughts; how to form: Noun + だ + と思いました)]

クレイさんは面白い言葉だと思いました。

あるひ、にほんじん　の　ともだち　と　しょっぴんぐ　もーる　に　いきました。

- ある日 aru hi—one day; (on) a certain day [ある (a certain; some) + 日 (day)]

- 日本人の友達と nihonjin no tomodachi to—with a Japanese friend [日本人 (Japanese; Japanese person) + の (modifier) + 友達 (friend; companion) + と (with)]

- ショッピングモールに行きました shoppingu mo-ru ni ikimashita—went to a shopping mall [ショッピングモール (shopping mall) + に (to; expresses direction and destination) + 行きました (went; polite past form of 行く (to go))]

ある日、日本人の友達とショッピングモールに行きました。

あざらし　が　かかれた　おおきな　こうこく
が　ありました。

- アザラシが描かれた azarashi ga kakareta—with a seal (animal) drawn on (it) [アザラシ (seal (animal)) + が (emphasizes the preceding word) + 描かれた (was drawn; was painted; plain passive past form of 描く (to draw; to paint))]

- 大きな広告がありました ookina koukoku ga arimashita—there was a large advertisement [大きな (big; large; great) + 広告 (advertisement; advertising) + が (emphasizes the preceding word) + ありました (there was; polite past form of ある (there is; to have; to be; to exist))]

アザラシが描かれた大きな広告がありました。

くれいさん は それ を ゆびさして 「あざ らし！」と おおきな こえ で いいました。

- それを指差して sore o yubisashite—(Clay) pointed at it and [それ (it; that) + を (indicates the direct object of action) + 指差 して (pointed at and; て-form of 指差す (to point at) which is used to connect to the next phrase, creating the meaning of "and")]

- 大きな声で ookina koe de—loudly; in a loud voice [大きな (big; loud) + 声 (voice) + で (in)]

- 「アザラシ！」と大きな声で言いました 「azarashi!」to ookina koe de iimashita—said loudly, 「アザラシ！」[「アザ ラシ」("アザラシ (sea (animal))"; 「」 (quotation marks; " ")) + と (quotation marker; used for quoting (thoughts, speech, etc.)) + 大きな声で (loudly; in a loud voice) + 言いました (said; polite past form of 言う (to say; to utter))]

クレイさんはそれを指差して 「アザラシ！」と 大きな声で言いました。

すると、くれいさん の にほんじん の ともだち は、「どうして そんな ことば を しって いる の？ すご～い！！」

- すると suru to—then; and

- クレイの日本人の友達は kurei no nihonjin no tomodachi wa—Clay's Japanese friend [クレイ (Clay) + の ('s; of; modifier) + 日本人 (Japanese; Japanese person) + 友達 (friend; companion) + は (indicates the sentence topic)]

- どうしてそんな言葉を知っているの？ doushite sonna kotoba o shitte iru no?—How do you know such word? [どうして (how; in what way; by what means) + そんな (such; that sort of; that kind of; like that) + 言葉 (word; term) + を (indicates the direct object of action) + 知っている (know; ている-form of 知る (to know; to be aware (of)) which is used to describe a continuous action; how to form: Verb て-form + いる) + の (question marker)]

- すご～い sugo~i—amazing; great; wonderful

すると、クレイさんの日本人の友達は、「どうして　そんな言葉を知っているの？すご～い！！」

と、とても　かんしん　した　ようす　でした。
この　あざらし　の　おかげ　で、くれいさん
の　もちべーしょん　が　あがりました。

- と to—(quotation marker; used for quoting speech)

- とても感心した様子でした totemo kanshin shita yousu deshita—seemed very impressed [とても (very; exceedingly) + 感心した (was/were impressed; plain past form of 感心する (be impressed; feel admiration; admire)) + 様子 (appearance; look(s); manner) + でした (was/were; polite past tense marker for nouns and な-adjectives)]

- このアザラシのおかげで kono azarashi no okage de—thanks to this アザラシ [この (this) + アザラシ (azarashi; seal (animal)) + のおかげで (thanks to; owing to; because of ~; how to form: Noun + の + おかげで)]

- クレイのモチベーションが上がりました kurei no mochibe-shon ga agarimashita—Clay's motivation increased [クレイ (Clay) + の ('s; of; modifier) + モチベーション (motivation) + が (identifies what performs the action) + 上がりました (increased; polite past form of 上がる (to increase; to go up; to rise))]

と、とても感心した様子でした。このアザラシ
のおかげで、クレイさんのモチベーションが上が
りました。

そして、いま　でも　にほんご　の　べんきょう
を　つづけて　います。

- そして soshite—and; and then

- 今でも ima demo—even now [今 (now; the present time) + でも (even; as well; also)]

- 日本語の勉強を続けています nihongo no benkyou o tsuzukete imasu—(he) continues to study Japanese [日本語 (Japanese (language)) + の (of; modifier) + 勉強 (study) + を (indicates the direct object of action) + 続けています (continue; continuing; ています-form of 続ける (to continue; to keep up; to keep on) which is used to describe an ongoing action; how to form: Verb て-form + います)]

そして、今でも日本語の勉強を続けています。

あなた　も　なにか　もちべーしょん　の　あが
る　ことば　を　ぜひ　みつけて　ください。

- あなたも anata mo—you too [あなた (you) + も (too; also; as well)]

- 何<small>なに</small>かモチベーションの上<small>あ</small>がる言葉<small>ことば</small> nanika mochibe-shon no agaru kotoba—some words that motivate (you) [何<small>なに</small>か (some; any; something) + モチベーション (motivation) + の (of; modifier) + 上<small>あ</small>がる (to increase; to go up; to rise) + 言葉 (word; term)]

- ぜひ zehi—please; do; certainly

- 見<small>み</small>つけてください mitsukete kudasai—find; please find [from 見<small>み</small>つける (to find; to discover; to come across); ~てください is used when requesting, instructing, ordering someone to do something; how to form: Verb て-form + ください]

あなたも何<small>なに</small>かモチベーションの上<small>あ</small>がる言葉<small>ことば</small>をぜ
ひ見<small>み</small>つけてください。

REVIEW

Now, review core vocabulary before trying to read the story in natural Japanese (no furigana or spaces).

- モチベーション *mochibe-shon*—motivation

- とても大切 *totemo taisetsu*—very important [とても (very; exceedingly) + 大切 (important; significant)]

- 日本語 *nihongo*—Japanese (language)

- 勉強 *benkyou*—study

- 新しい *atarashii*—new; recent; latest

- アザラシ *azarashi*—seal (animal)

- 言葉 *kotoba*—word; phrase; term

- 単語 *tango*—word; vocabulary

- 辞書 *jisho*—dictionary

- 覚える *oboeru*—to learn; to acquire; to memorize

- 日常会話 *nichijou kaiwa*—everyday conversation

- あまり *amari*—(not) very; (not) much

- 面白い *omoshiroi*—interesting; fascinating; intriguing

- 日本人の友達 *nihonjin no tomodachi*—Japanese friend
  [日本人 (Japanese; Japanese person) + の (modifier) + 友達 (friend; companion)]

- ショッピングモール *shoppingu mo-ru*—shopping mall

- 広告 *koukoku*—advertisement

- 声 *koe*—voice

- すごい *sugoi*—amazing; great; wonderful

- あなた *anata*—you

- 上がる *agaru*—to increase; to go up;

THE STORY

Now, let's read the story once more in natural Japanese.

モチベーションはとても大切です。

クレイさんが日本語を勉強し始めたばかりの頃、「新しい」という言葉を覚えました。辞書を見ると、「新しい」の前にあったのが「アザラシ ((the animal) seal)」という言葉でした。そこで、これを覚えることにしました。

「新しいアザラシ」と何度も言いながら、２つの単語を覚えました。「新しい」と「アザラシ」の２つです。「アザラシ」という言葉は日常会話ではあまり使わないかもしれませんが、クレイさんは面白い言葉だと思いました。

ある日、日本人の友達とショッピングモールに行きました。アザラシが描かれた大きな広告がありました。

クレイさんはそれを指差して「アザラシ！」と大きな声で言いました。

　すると、クレイさんの日本人の友達は、「どうしてそんな言葉を知っているの？すご〜い！！」と、とても感心した様子でした。

　このアザラシのおかげで、クレイさんのモチベーションが上がりました。そして、今でも日本語の勉強を続けています。

　あなたも何かモチベーションの上がる言葉をぜひ見つけてください。

ENGLISH

Motivation is very important.

When Clay first started studying Japanese, he learned the word "新しい (new)." When he looked in the dictionary, the word 「新しい (new)」 was preceded by the word 「アザラシ (the animal seal).」 So he decided to learn it.

He learned the two words by saying 「新しいアザラシ」 over and over again. The word 「アザラシ」 may not be used in everyday conversation, but Clay thought it was an interesting word.

One day, he went to a shopping mall with a Japanese friend. There was a large advertisement with a seal (animal) on it. Clay pointed at it and said loudly, 「アザラシ!」

Then Clay's Japanese friend said, "How do you know that word? Amazing!", and seemed very impressed.

Thanks to this アザラシ, Clay's motivation increased. And he continues to study Japanese even now.

Please find some words that motivate you too.

Thank you

We hope this has helped demystify basic Japanese sentence structure. If you have any questions or need clarification as you go through this material, don't hesitate to reach out to us at help@thejapanshop.com.

If you enjoyed the style of this book, we invite you to consider becoming a Makoto+ member. As a member, you'll receive our monthly Makoto e-zine, along with near-daily exclusive lessons that include comprehensive explanations and audio support.

https://MakotoPlus.com

Lastly, be sure to check out our other money-saving digital bundles at:

https://www.TheJapanShop.com/bundles

DOWNLOAD LINK

Please go to this website to download the sound files for all stories: (There is an exclusive *free* **gift on kanji** waiting there too.)

http://japanesereaders.com/ym4a

Thank you for purchasing and reading this book! To contact the authors, please email them at help@thejapanshop.com.

See also the wide selection of materials for learning Japanese at www.TheJapanShop.com and the free site for learning Japanese at www.TheJapanesePage.com.

Made in the USA
Columbia, SC
14 August 2024

39985282R00070